"What I admire most about Dr. Ayala's book, Journey Through Divorce, is that her main premise is based on having a "healthy" divorce, taking into account the best interest of the children. In simple style, she explains the complicated new divorce laws in Illinois. As a social scientist, I completely agree with her "3Cs" recipe for making the divorce process less painful: Communication, Cooperation and Collaboration. I highly recommend this book to anyone who is considering to dissolve his/her marriage without breaking the bank -- in terms of time, emotional effort and financial resources."

- DR. YOLANDA AYUBI
Global Communications Consultant

"Dr. Ayala succinctly explains the divorce legal web and offers tangible and realistic options for those seeking a wholesome life."

- KEITH COLEMAN
Volunteer Business Mentor

"Journey Through Divorce, Doris Ayala's first of a three-book series, is a wonderful start for those who are going through the divorce process. She lists five reasons to read this powerful guide, but the most important one is 'you will feel better prepared to make informed decisions'. Journey Through Divorce is written in a simple and understandable language and provides the necessary information to go through an uncontested divorce. A must-read for those going through this process. Thank you Dr. Ayala for putting this out there!"

- CAROLINA HERRERA
Author

Journey Through Divorce

A Guide to Your Rights and Options for a Healthy Divorce in Illinois

DORIS N. AYALA, PhD, MJ.

Journey Through Divorce

© Copyright 2017, Doris N. Ayala, PhD, MJ
All rights reserved.

No portion of this book may be reproduced by mechanical, photographic or electronic process, nor may it be stored in a retrieval system, transmitted in any form or otherwise be copied for public use or private use without written permission of the copyright owner.

This book is designed for general information purposes only. The information presented herein should not be construed to be formal legal advice. References are provided for informational purposes only and do not constitute endorsement of any websites or other sources. Readers should be aware that the websites listed in this book may change.

Cover Design & Layout by Doris N. Ayala and Juan Pablo Ruiz

ISBN: 978-0-9971605-3-6

This book series is dedicated to all those who experience unanticipated life changes, but who struggle to regain their footing for a brighter future for themselves and their families.

Contents

Acknowledgments VIII

Preface IX

Introduction X

1. Divorce Under the New Illinois Marriage and 1
Dissolution of Marriage Act (Senate Bill 57)

2. Current Statistics on Divorce 3

3. Petitioning for Divorce, Annulment, or Legal Separation 5

4. In the Best Interest of the Child(ren) 15

5. Communication, Cooperation, and Collaboration 23

6. The Psychological Impact of Divorce 27

7. Conclusion 33

5 Reasons Why You Should Read This Guide

1. You will acquire the knowledge of the marital dissolution law as it has recently changed.

2. You will avoid the pitfalls of the legal system.

3. You will feel better prepared to make informed decisions.

4. You will tread courageously through the challenging process of divorce.

5. You will learn how to better navigate through divorce to meet your needs and your children's needs.

Acknowledgments

There are numerous individuals to thank, not least of which are the many who willingly gave their time and shared their thoughtful insights into how to pursue writing a book, one that would benefit the many contemplating divorce.

I wish to thank my writers group, Katherine Akbar and Michele Kelly, for their editorial assistance on this project. I thank Jackie Camacho's inspiring dialogue and whose own story led me to think that I can offer something of value to readers.

As always, I am indebted to the support and encouragement of my staff, Yolanda Perez and Karen Ledezma, who always go the extra mile to ensure that I have not forgotten something, had time to complete a report, and have maintained a highly efficient office. I thank my clients for the many lessons they have taught me throughout the years and who serve as the impetus for this project.

I thank my children Lariza, Jose Antonio, Armando and Cristina who continue to believe in my capacity to be a dynamic woman as I embrace my future by exploring new possibilities and living a personally meaningful, busy lifestyle.

Last but not least, I thank my life partner, Dr. Walter A. Pedemonte, for being so patient and mindful of my ongoing life goals as I persevere in surmounting the challenges and obstacles I continue to face.

Preface
by: Megan Lopp Mathias

I am an attorney that represents women and minority business owners in business disputes and family law disputes. I have the utmost respect for Dr. Ayala and her unique ability to utilize her skills as a divorce professional to allow divorcing couples to see the true end game. As a clinician and a mediator, Dr. Ayala is adept at assisting couples in addressing the issues that need to be tackled in order to allow resolution to evolve.

As a divorce professional, the skills Dr. Ayala has, and so eloquently demonstrates in this book, are necessary for couples to avoid the litigation process, which becomes more expensive, extensive and elusive. Dr. Ayala brings an element of trust and confidence to a process wrought with distrust and anxiety.

I have known Dr. Ayala for more than 10 years through our respective work for women and minorities in the Chicagoland area. We were both involved in Women in Management, Inc., a group that was focused on empowering women. In family law disputes, divorces, custody disputes and the like, one of the most critical issues is managing perceptions and the realistic potential outcomes of a case.

This book highlights the issues that divorcing couples in Illinois need to understand in order to come to a mutually acceptable resolution. In this book, Dr. Ayala methodically identifies critical facts regarding the process and the factors a couple needs to consider that relate to family law disputes. Dr. Ayala uses her many years of working with couples on conflict resolution in order to identify the baseline from which the couple should begin their discussions. The book also describes different proceedings, which can be utilized to avoid pure litigation. Her perspective is enlightening and empowering to couples looking down the long road of divorce.

Well done, Dr. Ayala!

Introduction

If you are reading these words right now, you are most likely considering a divorce or going through one. The miles in front of you may seem long. There are many unknowns. You might wonder how you are going to get through it all. One thing that can make the journey a little brighter and a little easier is knowledge. That is why I am authoring a series of three guidebooks to help individuals and couples who are thinking about ending a marriage but want to do so as amicably as possible.

When experiencing turmoil in our lives, we often wonder if our lives will get better—and how long it will take to feel relieved, relaxed and moving out of the depths of our despair. Divorce is a unique kind of turmoil. When the fabric of a marriage begins to fray and divorce becomes an option, no matter the trigger, it becomes a life-changing state of affairs not only for the couple but for the nuclear family, extended family, friends and acquaintances as well.

Journey Through Divorce is the first of three guidebooks. Here, we focus on divorce laws in Illinois and important factors to consider when taking the steps toward divorce. You will need to make important decisions and having the knowledge will make it easier to navigate the legal system and your future.

The second book explains the process of divorce and how to make it as easy and trouble-free as possible. This guide will show you steps on how to better cope with the stressors you encounter; for example: parenting responsibilities, parenting arrangements and plans as well as considering financial obligations that may impact you and your family.

Lastly, the third book teaches individuals how to see divorce as part of a larger picture so you can navigate life in a healthy way. You will consider ongoing issues you will most likely continue to cope with and face the "what happens next" part of your life—after a divorce when you find yourself single or living as a single parent. You'll read inspiring stories by real people. Their telescope offers up a view "beyond the horizon" that is both encouraging and informative.

1 DIVORCE UNDER THE NEW ILLINOIS MARRIAGE AND DISSOLUTION OF MARRIAGE ACT
(Senate Bill 57)

Divorce is the legal dissolution of a marital union. It dissolves the bonds of matrimony between a married couple under the laws of the state in which the couple live in. The Illinois Marriage and Dissolution of Marriage Act (IMDMA) has made some significant changes that individuals contemplating divorce need to know.

The revised Illinois Marriage and Dissolution of Marriage Act (IMDMA 5/401) went into effect on January 1, 2016. This is the first time since 1996 that the marriage law in Illinois has been amended to reflect national trends in family law. Among the major changes, the revised law makes the no-fault divorce process easier and eliminates the words "custody" and "visitation," focusing instead on shared parenting responsibilities.

NO-FAULT DIVORCE

Fifty years ago, people who wanted to get a divorce needed to prove to the court that their spouses engaged in behaviors warranting a dissolution of marriage. In the early 1970s, Illinois law introduced the "no-fault divorce," enabling parties to file for divorce for nonspecific reasons known as "irreconcilable differences."

In 1970 the law was updated but still required that the couple be separated for at least two years before filing for a no-fault divorce. The parties could reduce that time to six months if both of them signed a waiver. Since the 1970s, Illinois law permitted divorces not only for irreconcilable differences but also adultery, impotency, and habitual drunkenness, to name a few. The revised IMDMA eliminated all other grounds for divorce except for irreconcilable differences. This process differs considerably from the old law and reflects more modern, efficient divorce practices.

According to the IMDMA (5/401), individuals must show that irreconcilable differences have caused the irretrievable breakdown of the marriage. The court determines that efforts at reconciliation have failed or that future attempts at reconciliation would be impracticable and not in the best interest of the family. Under the revised IMDMA, couples only have to live apart for a minimum of six months before the entry of judgment dissolving the marriage (not the initial filing) proves irreconcilable differences. Therefore, both the required separation period and the method of calculation of that period shortens the total time before a divorce may take place.

Additionally, the revised law requires the court to enter its judgment within 60 days of the parties completing their presentation of evidence and/or testimony to the court (called the "closing of proofs"), or after a trial.

"Divorce is a time of change. It really rocks a foundation of most people's lives. When we have our heart broken or our dreams taken away from us, it is a time of growth and change."
- Debbie Ford

2 CURRENT STATISTICS ON DIVORCE

The concept of divorce has evolved from something unthinkable, disgraceful or even scandalous to something that many individuals experience—personally or through friends or family. Although the stigma against divorce continues, the parting of ways between two married people is more common than ever, with approximately one million couples in the United States getting divorced every year. Researchers who collect data on divorce may present different numbers based on the methods they use. Many scholars continue to cite the generally accepted "40% to 50%" statistic although data shows that the divorce rate has been declining since the 1990s. Still, this doesn't mean that there is less conflict amongst couples; rather, there are more couples cohabitating before marriage, which helps them to determine whether they will tie the knot in later years. Other reasons include the economic recession and women's educational opportunities leading to self-sustaining careers and greater independence. Marriage patterns differ markedly by age at marriage and by educational attainment as well as by racial/ethnic groups.

The cultural tolerance for divorce grows, however. According to the Gallup poll in 2008 Values and Beliefs survey, up to 70% of Americans showed that they believe that divorce is morally acceptable, which included those Americans who stated that religion is very important in their lives. In a 2014 survey conducted by Statista, adult Americans show divorce to be acceptable—27% are very acceptable and 31% showed to be somewhat acceptable. A survey conducted by Statista in 2016, 72% of Americans stated that divorce is morally acceptable.

These statistics demonstrate that the political and personal landscape is changing drastically.

Many people who get divorced remarry, but those marriages have an even lower rate of success with 67% of second marriages ending in divorce. The divorce rates for third marriages are even higher, proving that the third doesn't always work either. In Cook County alone, 45,376 couples got divorced between 2011 and 2014 (Circuit Court of Cook County, 2015).

When a couple has tried everything they can to save the marriage, and they're still not happy with each other, the best choice for everyone involved may be divorce. Many couples with children try to stay together "for the sake of the children"; however, children rarely benefit from an environment of parental discord. Dissolving the marriage can often lead to healthier, happier parents and children, especially if the divorce is amicable.

More recently, attention has been given to rising divorce rates for people over 40. Late-life divorce (also called "silver" or "gray" divorce) is becoming more common and culturally acceptable. In 2014, people aged 50+ were twice as likely to divorce than in 1990, according to the National Center for Family and Marriage Research at Bowling Green State University in Ohio. For individuals over 65, the increase was even higher. The AARP study, "The Divorce Experience: A Study of Divorce at Midlife and Beyond" (May 2004), showed that the major reason for more late-life divorce is the increasing financial independence of women, who initiate about 66% of divorces after age 40.

"Some people believe holding on and hanging in there are signs of great strength. However, there are times when it takes much more strength to know when to let go and then do it."
- Ann Landers

3 PETITIONING FOR DIVORCE, ANNULMENT OR LEGAL SEPARATION

UNCONTESTED DIVORCE

A divorce is "uncontested" when both parties accept to divorce. Uncontested divorces tend to be completed much more quickly than contested divorces. They can be finalized after only a brief hearing, and only the party who filed the petition for divorce is required to attend. The judge will ask questions to clarify your agreements, including that your marriage is not savable, and create a record of your responses.

When both parties agree to the divorce, they may file a Joint Petition for Simplified Dissolution of Marriage, provided they meet the residency requirement—living in Illinois for at least 90 days before one of the parties files for divorce, completion of the Petition for Dissolution of Marriage paperwork, and any spousal and child support. The couple works together and negotiates in dividing marital property and assigning debt accrued during the marriage in a mutually satisfactory way. Couples are encouraged to seek help from a financial advisor if they have concerns about the division of property and assets.

Advantages To Choosing An Uncontested Divorce

- It can often provide couples with a dissolution process that involves much less drama, confrontation and conflict than months or years litigating in court;

- Couples may be on friendly and reasonable terms and emotionally capable of ending their marriage without dispute and drawn out negotiation;
- There are benefits for the divorcing couple not only at an emotional level, but financial as well, as the need for a court trial is unnecessary and keeps costs to both parties at a minimum;
- Uncontested divorces can be expedited through the court system within 60 days, preventing a drawn out process that is emotionally harmful to both parties and their children;
- Uncontested divorces are the simplest and easiest divorces to process. They do not, as a rule, require legal counsel for either party; however, when individuals are wary of the legal system they can obtain professional divorce services to assist them through the process from start to finish;
- When children are involved, the parents have the opportunity to decide on the parenting responsibilities and plan child support in an amicable manner;
- It is relatively inexpensive.

Reasons Not To Choose Uncontested Divorce

- When the couple is experiencing a high level of conflict and is not in agreement with distribution of assets, the child responsibilities plan and child support;
- When the communication between the couple has broken down;
- When the couple has real estate properties, joint bank accounts and assets which may create conflict when deciding to settle;
- When there is domestic violence and the victim needs an advocate to represent her/him.

COLLABORATIVE DIVORCE

Collaborative Divorce is a family law process that provides couples with avenues for dealing with legal disputes. The couple agrees to work out a settlement without going to court, except at the end when the couple finalizes the divorce process and stands before the judge. The benefits of a collaborative divorce are:

- There are attorneys, mediators, child specialists, divorce coaches, financial advisors, and mental health professionals available to assist couples in resolving any conflict that arises in settling issues;
- It reduces attorney and professional fees;
- It gives the couple control over all aspects of their cases.

Each party can decide whether to hire an attorney to represent him or herself, but the attorneys serve in a collaborative, non-adversarial capacity. In this case, the attorneys may use a lot of the same techniques used by mediators in order to constructively facilitate communication between the parties. An attorney hired in a collaborative capacity can help keep everyone courteous, respectful and on track with the goal of reaching the divorce without conflict. Before going forward, everyone involved needs to abide by certain ground rules. The first is that all parties must treat the others involved with respect in order to maintain communication and cooperation. Respect, honesty and trust are also important components in a collaborative divorce.

CONTESTED DIVORCE

A contested divorce is an option more frequently chosen by individuals because it is the traditional or conventional model of divorce. Choosing this option becomes even more important when a couple is not in agreement on the division of assets and liabilities, alimony payments, and child parenting and support. This option requires that both parties hire attorneys who are skilled in negotiating these issues, where they then compromise and agree to a reasonable settlement. Disputed issues can be resolved by negotiations or by a series of hearings before the divorce trial. Living arrangements, parental responsibilities, and division of assets are common points of contention.

Thus, if the two parties do not agree to divorce, the party who filed the petition for divorce may include a list of allegations against his or her spouse in the pleadings. The parties will engage in "discovery," the process by which both parties obtain information about the marriage, including finances, evidence of certain allegations, etc. Discovery usually includes depositions (interviews used to gather information that may help the court determine the fairness of the division of assets, etc.) by one or both parties.

If the parties do not live in the same state, the divorce can be filed in the state in which the filing party lives, as long as that person has lived there at least 90 days. The other party must be notified and given an opportunity to respond within 30 days of the filing. This is done when the person filing for divorce provides the information of where the other party lives and they are served with the legal documents.

Couples should weigh this option carefully and seriously. For many, this form of divorce becomes a very adversarial process, financially costly (reducing marital assets, future earning capacity adversely affecting the best interest of the children, etc.), and highly emotionally charged, which may be psychologically detrimental to everyone involved.

MILITARY DIVORCE

The rules of divorce differ somewhat for those who serve in the military and their respective spouses.

For example, because military families oftentimes find themselves moving or one spouse being called to serve in another part of the world, the "Uniformed Services Former Spouses' Protection Act" (USFSPA) is a federal law that gives power to the state of residence. According to *Stateside Legal*, the law stipulates: "The state where the military member resides always has the power to divide the military pension in a divorce. So if you file for divorce in a state that is not the military member's state of legal residence, then the court may not have the authority to divide the pension."

Other areas of difference include: calculation of support amounts, parenting plan and responsibilities, court time scheduling and deadlines, pension rights, and benefit allotments. Typically, military legal assistance lawyers cannot represent you or your spouse in a divorce, but they can be a wealth of information for knowing the unique aspects of military divorces.

PUBLICATION DIVORCE

If one spouse wants to end a marriage but the other spouse cannot be found, a "publication divorce" may be permitted. In this case, the spouse must be able to show that s/he made reasonable efforts to locate the other person, including publishing a notice in a newspaper of general circulation informing that person of divorce proceedings ("service by publication"). If the missing spouse does not respond to the publication, the filing party may win by default.

A court will only grant a publication divorce to someone who submits a completed "affidavit of diligent search," which proves the filing party conducted a "good faith search" for the spouse. Under Illinois law, a "good faith search" means the spouse searched the Internet, phone books, and directory assistance in the areas where the other spouse may live and was last known to have lived. Additionally, the spouse must also be able to show that s/he asked friends and relatives, checked the post office for a forwarding address, and sought information from the tax collector, landlords, prior employers, and the registrar of voters.

The published notice of divorce proceedings must appear in three successive weekly publications in the county in which the divorce is being sought. Note, however, that in the event that the spouse is located, a petition for a divorce by publication is no longer an option.

A DECLARATION OF INVALIDITY OF MARRIAGE

According to the IMDMA (750 ILCS 5/301-306), a Declaration of Invalidity of Marriage (formerly known as an annulment) declares that a marriage never really existed. Illinois does not have an official court action called "annulment of marriage," but a spouse can request an equivalent called a *"judgment of invalidity."* As the name suggests, a judgment of invalidity is a final order stating that the marriage was never valid. The criteria for a judgment of invalidity include the following:

- One of the spouses lacked the capacity to consent to the marriage because, at the time the marriage was made official, the spouse was suffering from a mental problem or infirmity or because the spouse was under the influence of alcohol or other intoxicating drugs.
- One spouse agreed to the marriage only because of force, fraud, or duress (coercion). For fraud to be a viable ground for annulment, the fraud has to affect the heart of the marriage. For example, if Spouse A lied about personal wealth, that would not be enough of a fraud to allow annulment. But if Spouse A never intended to live with Spouse B and only got married to avoid deportation, Spouse B could apply for annulment.
- One of the spouses lacks the physical capacity to consummate the marriage through sexual intercourse and at the time they married the other spouse did not know of the incapacity.
- The marriage is legally prohibited because it is bigamous (meaning, one spouse is still legally married to another living person) or incestuous (the spouses are closely related by blood or adoption).
- One of the spouses was aged 16 or 17 at the time of marriage and did not have the approval of a parent, guardian, or have judicial approval.

Before asking for a judgment of invalidity, the individual needs to be aware of certain "statutes of limitations" (legal deadlines). These limitations include the following:

- If mental incapacity, intoxication, fraud, duress, or force are at issue, then either spouse must file for a judgment of invalidity no later than 90 days after the petitioner gained knowledge of the complaint they are presenting.
- If physical incapacity is the issue, the spouse may file no later than one year after learning about the impotency.
- If youth is the issue, the underage spouse or the spouse's parent or guardian must file before the underage spouse reaches the legal age of marriage—18 years old in Illinois. However, the age of consent for sexual contact is 17 years old. This law was established to protect youth engaging in a sexual relationship from prosecution.
- If bigamy is the issue, either the spouse, the States Attorney, or a child of either party may file for a judgment of invalidity not to exceed three years after the death of the first spouse to die.

LEGAL SEPARATION

A legal separation is similar to a divorce but does not terminate the marital relationship and the couple cannot remarry. Illinois law recognizes legal separation but because the process, specifically the expense and the outcome, are similar to those of divorce, people usually opt for staying married but not living together or they eventually decide to get a divorce.

According to the IMDMA (705 ILCS 5/401), the court grants the couple an official way to live separate lives, while working out the financial and/or emotional details that may be important to preserve (for example, a spouse may have a terminal illness or the spouses want to continue filing taxes together). The couple receives a judicial decree formally requiring that the couple live apart. Illinois grants a separation for an unlimited amount of time. If the couple wants to get divorced, they will go through the process of petitioning for a divorce. In Illinois, either spouse can decide to end the marriage even if the other spouse does not want to get a divorce.

Here's a brief story that shows how separation proved to be the most logical choice;

S and T married 30 years ago. S suffered much hardship with her husband who was an alcoholic and at times a drug user. Within the past five years S decided to separate from her husband. She now receives social security and other benefits that the spouse was entitled to.

"And once the storm is over you won't remember how you made it through, how you managed to survive. You won't even be sure, in fact, whether the storm is really over. But one thing is certain. When you come out of the storm you won't be the same person who walked in."
- Haruki Murakami

4 IN THE BEST INTEREST OF THE CHILD(REN)

Parenting is one of the most important jobs that a person may ever have. Children depend on their parents to guide them safely and lovingly to adulthood. After separation or divorce, parenting can be more challenging but your children's basic and special needs don't change. When couples with children divorce they need to focus and work on ensuring the best interest of their child(ren). This means that the parent's ultimate goals are to foster and encourage the child's safety, physical, developmental, moral, mental and psychological well-being into young adulthood.

The revised law has substituted the term "custody" with "parental responsibility" and the term "visitation" with "allocating the parental responsibility." Time spent with the children by either parent is now referred to as "parenting time."

Under the old law, custodial parents (ones with the primary custody of the children) had all parental decision-making authority. Sometimes a custodial parent would be required to confer with the other parent, but the custodial parent ultimately decided major parenting issues.

Under the revised IMDMA, parental decision-making authority can be divided between two parents regardless of which parent has primary parental responsibilities. This revised law requires a parenting plan that delineates parenting responsibilities, parenting schedules, and children's living arrangements. The parents may agree on this plan privately, or if the parents don't come up with an acceptable plan the court may determine the parenting plan after a hearing. The plan also includes a mediation provision, which provides a way for the parties to address any parenting conflicts or changes after the divorce is finalized.

When determining parental responsibilities, the court's chief concern has always been the best interests of the child. This priority remains unchanged under the IMDMA, but the revised law offers innovative methods to determine "best interests." To determine parental responsibility (formerly known as custody), Illinois courts used to consider how active each parent was in child-rearing at the time of the divorce. However, many parents felt that the other parent did little or nothing with the children until the divorce was filed, at which point s/he suddenly became active.

In order to solve this problem, the IMDMA requires the court to consider how much time each parent spent taking care of the children for a full two years before the divorce was filed. (If the child is less than two years old, then the court evaluates the time period from the child's birth to the filing of the divorce.) This method gives the court a clearer idea of each family's normal parenting situation for parental responsibility determinations. The court also takes into account situations of conflict where parents may not always be objective or capable of deciding the best arrangements.

Section 602 of the Illinois Divorce Act (IMDMA, 750 ILCS 5/602) stipulates what the court views as important in determining allocation of responsibilities. Key factors in the decision-making are as follows:

- The wishes of the child's parent or parents as to his custody;
- The wishes of the child as to his custodian;
- The interaction and interrelationship of the child with his parent or parents, his siblings and any other person who may significantly affect the child's best interest;
- The child's adjustment to his home, school, and community;
- The mental and physical health of all individuals involved;
- The physical violence or threat of physical violence by the child's potential custodian, whether directed against the child or directed against another person;
- The occurrence of ongoing abuse, whether directed against the child or directed against another person;
- The willingness and ability of each parent to facilitate and encourage a close and continuing relationship between the other parent and the child;
- Whether one of the parents is a sex offender; and
- The terms of a parent's military family-care plan that a parent must complete before deployment if a parent is a member of the United States Armed Forces.

Additionally, the revised law requires the court to consider how capable each parent is of putting the child's needs before his/her own needs. Previously, divorce courts unevenly applied best interests evaluations. The revised law has created a uniform standard for all courts to consider these factors in every divorce.

One of the biggest benefits of the "parenting responsibility" concept is that child-related decisions are less win/lose. Parents no longer "win" or "lose" custody. Instead, each parent may be allocated certain important parental responsibilities, regardless of how much time s/he spends with the child. This divisional approach is intended to result in less violence and animosity between the parents, creating a happier divorce and a healthier environment for the children.

In the interests of trying to keep families together as much as possible, Illinois law previously prohibited one parent from moving across state lines with the child without court approval. The revised law allows parents to relocate with the child (Sec.5/600). The parent that is relocating must provide (at least 60 days before moving) a written notice to the court with information on when he/she will leave, for how long and the parent's new address. If the other parent objects, a petition will have to be submitted to the court. The court will ultimately decide based on the following factors:

- The circumstances and reason for the relocation;
- The reasons, if any, that the other parent is objecting to the relocation;
- The history and quality of each parent's relationship with the child(ren); the educational opportunities in the existing and new location;
- The presence or absence of extended family; the anticipated impact of the relocation on the child(ren);
- Whether the court will be able to fashion a reasonable allocation of parental responsibilities between the parents;
- The wishes of the child—taking into account the child's maturity;
- Possible arrangements for the exercise of parental responsibilities appropriate to the parents' resources and circumstances, and the development level of the child;
- Minimization of the impairment to a parent-child relationship caused by the parent's relocation; and
- Any other relevant factors bearing on the child's best interests.

Certain Illinois counties even allow parents to move as far as 50 miles away without seeking court approval. If the moving parent violates the relocation laws, Illinois maintains jurisdiction to oversee the resolution of this issue. The revised law still makes an effort to keep families together but loosened the restrictions on where separated parents can live.

CHILD SUPPORT

Modifications to the IMDMA effective July 1, 2017
750ILCS 5/505 and 750ILCS 5/510

This chaper clarifies information on the current child support laws and informs the reader the amended sections 505 and 510 of the Illinois Marriage and Dissolution of Marriage Act (IMDMA) that will take effect on July 1, 2017.

Please note that Illinois Governor Rauner signed into law Public Act 99-0746 which amends the IMDMA by changing sections 505 and 510 with regards to the child support law. The revised law replaces the existing child support guidelines (as outlined in this book) to one with an "income shares" model. At the core of this model is a schedule of basic obligations that reflects child-rearing expenditures for a range of combined parental incomes and number of children. Thus, the new law shows how the child should receive the same amount of parental income that he or she would have received if the parents lived together. A big advantage to this change is that when both parents work and receive an income this change makes both parents responsible for contributing to the support of the child as stipulated in the new guidelines.

Although the revised law at this time has done away with the terms "custody" and "visitation," the provisions regarding child support remain mostly unchanged. The court may order either or both parents "owing a duty of support" to the child to pay a reasonable and necessary amount. The "duty of support" includes the obligation to provide for the reasonable and necessary educational, physical, mental, and emotional health needs of the child. The term "child" includes any child under age 18 and any child under age 19 who is still attending high school (750 ILC.S 5/505).

The court determines the minimum amount of support owed by parents to their children by applying the following net income guidelines:

Number of Children	Percent of Parent's Net Income
1	20%
2	28%
3	32%
4	40%
5	45%
6 or more	50%

The court will also take into account a series of other factors, such as the parent's financial resources, the child's educational needs, and the child's physical, emotional, and mental health needs, to name a few.

If the court finds that a deviation from the guidelines is appropriate after considering the best interest of the child(ren), the court will then set the child support based on its findings and may order either or both parents to pay child support.

NON-MINOR CHILD SUPPORT

Traditionally, the obligation to pay child support ended when the child turned 18 or graduated from high school, whichever came last. However, as the costs of higher education continue to rise, the law was adjusted to take this factor into account. Illinois now requires both parents to contribute to the child's educational expenses until the child reaches the age of 23 or attains a bachelor's degree (750 ILCS 5/513). This is not only for a college education but extends to vocational or professional or other training after graduation from high school. If someone can show "good cause" (justification) as to why both parents should continue to provide educational expenses after that point, contribution can be extended until the child turns 25.

Alternatively, the amount a parent will have to contribute to a child's education, rather than the duration, can be used to determine when a parent no longer has to contribute. The new IMDMA limits the cost to the equivalent of an education at the University of Illinois. The law also gives the parent the right to access the child's transcripts, grade reports, etc. If the child's grade point average (GPA) falls below a "C", the parent will no longer be obligated to pay educational expenses, unless the child can prove illness or other good cause. Parents may also avoid contribution to education costs if the child obtains a bachelor's degree or gets married.

If the parents are unable to agree on supporting the non-minor child, the issue is presented to the court in a hearing where the judge then determines the allocation of the child's college expenses between both parents and the child.

Some aspects that the court takes into account are as follows:

- The parent's current and future financial resources;
- The child's standard of living if the parents had not divorced;
- The financial resources of the child;
- The child's academic performance; and
- Other factors that the court finds relevant to the case.

When parents do not comply with child support orders, Illinois provides for contempt and enforcement proceedings. If the court finds that a parent's noncompliance with the support order was willful and without justification, the court has the discretion to hold that parent (or both) in contempt and enter sanctions against the parent. Penalties may include:

- Placing the parent on probation;
- Sentencing the parent to periodic imprisonment;
- Ordering any part or all of the earnings of a parent during a sentence of imprisonment be paid to the Clerk of the Circuit Court or to the other parent receiving the support of the child(ren).

"At the end of the day, the most overwhelming key to a child's success is the positive involvement of parents."
- Jane D. Hull

5 COMMUNICATION, COOPERATION, AND COLLABORATION

Most people would agree that one of the keys to a successful marriage is communication. Unfortunately, not everyone has effective, diplomatic communication skills necessary to maintain a successful long-term relationship. When emotions run high, each party may find it difficult to hear and understand what the other is saying. Fights and heated discussions break out when one or both parties focus on defending their own actions rather than listening to what the other party has to say.

Effective communication can help protect a marriage from dissolving into divorce, but sometimes it is not enough. When a couple has reached the point where the marriage is no longer salvageable, the need to communicate and cooperate with each other becomes even more important for their peace of mind and for the successful outcome of divorce proceedings.

When most people think of divorce, they envision a couple and their lawyers at a table, bickering over assets and the children, if any, without speaking directly to each other or they envision an angry couple devaluing each other while not listening to reason. Those images alone are enough to make anyone groan and perhaps put off the thought of filing for divorce. However, not all divorces have that much animosity. In many cases, both parties agree to dissolve the marriage amicably, avoid going through litigation, and ask a judge to make decisions for them — which can be extremely costly, time-consuming, and overwhelming for everyone. The option of going through an uncontested divorce can be a very good choice.

Communication, cooperation, and collaboration are all key elements to making sure a divorce goes smoothly — with less tension and stress for all concerned. A divorce handled in this manner sounds great, but an amicable divorce can be easier said than done. Both parties need to agree to hear and address each other's thoughts, feelings, and concerns with respect. That can be difficult if one or both of the parties is still angry from the emotional effect of ending the marital relationship. Angry feelings may constitute a good reason for couples to hire attorneys to represent their interests in the divorce.

By communicating, collaborating, and cooperating with each other respectfully, divorcing couples save themselves a lot of time, money, stress, and heartache. A divorce in which both parties make an honest attempt to get along with each other during the divorce proceedings can help maintain their friendship throughout their child's life. Parents can collaborate closely by sharing clear goals through a structured system of discussion on an ongoing basis that can provide peaceful and positive action. Children will emerge from the experience happier, physically and mentally healthier, and more secure than children who are made to suffer through a bitter and hostile divorce and its aftermath.

Children learn how to behave in certain situations by modeling those around them, especially their parents. A divorce, in which each parent does his/her best to consider the other's needs, will teach the children about healthy dispute resolution. They will also recognize that, while their parents no longer choose to live with one another, they are not the cause or center of their parent's conflict.

The good news is that the vast majority of divorces (about 95%) are settled through mediation or other means without resorting to trial—this means the divorce is uncontested.

Oftentimes a spouse who is hurt and angry may wish to take the divorce to trial to make the other party pay for the pain s/he caused, but no one wins in that situation. Using communication and cooperation to come to a mutually acceptable arrangement is the best course of action for everyone involved. When a couple reaches an amicable agreement and wants to go with an uncontested divorce, professional divorce services that facilitate Pro Se divorce can be a cost-efficient way of handling the divorce as well as having someone work with them through the legal system.

It's important to keep in mind that information on social media platforms (Facebook, LinkedIn, Twitter, Instagram, YouTube, and Reddit, etc.) may be used as admissible evidence in court against the other spouse in a divorce proceeding. People have to remember that any texts, emails, messages, posts, or tweets to another person could come back to haunt them in court. Be sensible about how you communicate with others.

When a marital relationship has been irretrievably damaged, a divorce is often the only way for both parties to move forward. Recognizing this solution is the first step toward healing.

"When two people decide to get a divorce, it isn't a sign that they 'don't understand' one another, but a sign that they have, at last, begun to."
- Helen Rowland

6 THE PSYCHOLOGICAL IMPACT OF DIVORCE

THE CHILD(REN) OF DIVORCE

A divorce has a significant impact on everyone involved, especially children of the couple. Their world has turned upside down. Children often feel unprepared, sad, lonely, confused, anxious, and angry and may experience depression. Some kids will cope with the changes better than others. Separation and divorce means that children live in different homes, with different expectations and routines and it takes time for them to adjust. Children take their lead from their parents. If parents effectively communicate about how the separation and divorce will affect them and they maintain a healthy approach to coping with the events in their lives, children will learn to cope with their overwhelming emotions and they will experience less stress as they adjust to their diverse life circumstances.

According to the American Psychological Association (May 2004), children of divorced parents tend to have lower education levels, and therefore lower employment levels as adults. However, these findings may not be entirely due to the divorce itself. Children of divorced parents are also more likely to live in low-income homes, and their struggles may be due to financial challenges rather than divorce.

A recent study by Dr. Strohschein (2016), a sociologist at the University of Alberta in Canada, revealed that divorced parents do just as well at raising their children as a married couple. The study "revealed no differencee in nurturing, consistent or punitive parenting between the two groups of parents." Dr. Strohschein points out that children may already be having problems well before the divorce itself occurs because both family conflict and parental depression affect the child's mental health.

More recent studies on the effects of divorce on children show that children don't want to live with parents who are constantly fighting and devaluing each other. Children experience a great deal of stress when their parents have heated discussions and are unable to control their emotions. These children are often placed in the middle of these fights which can lead to their distancing themselves from the parents.

The good news: There are multiple things parents can do to limit the negative effects of divorce on their children. Chronic unresolved conflict between parents has been shown to result in greater emotional insecurity in children, suggesting that such parents should avoid exposing the children to a hostile separation and divorce process. Additionally, children who still have access to both parents during and after the divorce tend to have fewer emotional and behavioral problems. This is especially true when the children also receive appropriate parenting and experience low levels of conflict between the parents.

Access to grandparents and other close extended family members also play an important role in determining how well a child emerges from a divorce, although grandparents often get caught in the crossfire of divorce as well. However, if the parents maintain civil communication and allow the children to have access to both sets of grandparents (if they themselves aren't showing hostile behavior toward the other parent), the children benefit significantly.

THE DIVORCING INDIVIDUAL

All couples enter into marriage committing to a long-term relationship with hopes of maintaining a loving relationship throughout their time together. An interesting research article conducted by Ted Huston and his colleagues (2001) found that some couples have the seeds of unhappiness present from the very beginning—further showing that if the couple senses trouble in the relationship when it begins, it is probably a sign that the trouble will continue or worsen over time leading to divorce.

Even when a divorcing individual recognizes that separation serves the best interests of the family, s/he may experience depression, which may trigger unwanted thoughts, as well as a range of other emotions that will require mental health services. The five emotions most commonly associated with divorce are anger, guilt, fear, anxiety, and grief. Many people grieve the end of a marriage in much the same way they would if their spouse had died. Grief has its own stages, including denial, anger, bargaining, depression, and acceptance. Everyone deals with grief differently, and an individual may not experience the stages in the order above. For both men and women, endings can be difficult and painful, especially when they punctuate a life stage rooted in love.

After Sue and Frank's divorce was official, Sue expected to feel complete freedom and elation over her new life. She was resentful of Frank's affair and the pain he had caused her. His "other life" hurt her deeply; now it was over. After leaving the final proceedings where all the documents were signed, she went home, lay on the couch and cried. Her reaction shocked her, but it was, after all, an end.

A divorce can be especially traumatic for someone if one of the spouses did not expect or want the divorce. Some divorced partners experience low self-esteem, rejection, embarrassment, and/or a loss of identity. These feelings can be compounded if the divorce is accompanied by tense or hostile interactions with the spouse. Divorce is correlated with an increase in depressive episodes (depressed mood, loss of interest or pleasure in everyday activities, feelings of hopelessness and helplessness) affecting people who have a history of depression.

In a culture that discourages emotion from men, especially sadness and depression, many men have difficulty admitting their emotional struggles after divorce. Studies show that men are just as susceptible to the emotional trauma of divorce as women. It is important for both men and women to seek mental health services and develop a supportive system of friends and family, and/or health professionals.

FRIENDS AND FAMILIES

Divorce hits the couple and their children hardest, but they are not the only ones affected by the change. Extended family members and friends who have cultivated a relationship with the parties during the marriage may experience emotional pain, especially if the divorce becomes hostile.

When a couple gets married, each spouse's set of parents welcomes the new in-law into the family. They celebrate holidays, birthdays, and other important events together, developing strong bonds. When a couple decides to divorce, the entire family will need to adjust and also grieve the process.

Friends can also feel torn or upset when a couple separates. The divorcing pair may expect, and even pressure, their friends to take sides. For example, if one spouse cheated on or abandoned the other, the injured spouse may want to commiserate with friends. The hurt spouse may not only share feelings of pain and betrayal but may also be inclined to openly criticize or ridicule the other spouse, which can make long-time friends feel deeply uncomfortable. A Psychology Today survey found that divorcing couples typically had difficulty in maintaining their friendships with other couples (September 6, 2012). In most cases, a divorce results in coupled friends losing touch with at least one member of the divorced couple, occasionally both. Friendships are even more likely to end when one of the divorced parties moves to another neighborhood. Neighbors who were also friends suddenly become neither.

Furthermore, people going through a divorce may not feel comfortable around other couples, as seeing happily married friends can remind them of what they have lost. Likewise, coupled friends may feel uncomfortable around the divorcing pair for fear of offending them or being forced to choose sides. An open discussion about what each individual expects and needs is best for everyone involved.

On the other hand, single friends are more likely to maintain their relationships with one or both divorced parties. In some instances, people become closer to their single friends after a divorce.

"Because in every relationship there comes a point when the damage is too much and no matter how good it once was, the memories can't sustain you. You have to save yourself knowing all the while it hurts like hell, because you can't keep giving someone everything if you get nothing in return."
- Unknown

7 CONCLUSION

As we consider the past and the future we note that there have been profound social changes challenging the lives of so many families. Marriage was considered necessary to bear children and fulfill obligations. Divorce was inconceivable. As we examine these changes we take into account how marriage doesn't have the same functions and divorce becomes a solution for many. Our lives continue to shape us by the evolution of a progressive society. Every family is unique and a myriad of factors need to be weighed when making a decision to get a divorce.

Also to keep in mind is the assumption that parental divorce causes mental health problems in children, which has been challenged by more recent research. It has been found that many of the children who were part of earlier research showed to have been exposed to existing familial dysfunction and conflict way before the parents got divorced. Today, the effects of divorce can be considerably reduced when parents demonstrate goodwill towards each other and place the child's life as a priority in their lives.

REFERENCES

American Psychological Association (May, 2004) www.apa.org/about/gr/issues/cyf/divorce.aspx

Carrere, S. & Gottman, J.M.(1999). Predicting Divorce Among Newlyweds from the First Three Minutes of Marital Conflict Discussion, Family Process, Vol. 38(3), 293-301.

Circuit Court of Cook County. 2015. Clerk of the Circuit Court, Domestic Relations Division, Cook County. Data from 2011 thru 2014.

GALLUP: Saad, L. (May, 2008).Cultural Tolerance for Divorce Grows to 70%. www.gallup.com/poll/107380/cultural-tolerance -divorce-grows-70.aspx

Huston, T. L., Caughlin, J. P., Houts, R. M., Smith, S. E., & George, L. J. (2001). The connubial crucible: Newlywed years as predictors of marital delight, distress, and divorce. Journal of Personality and Social Psychology, 80(2), 237-252.

Illinois Marriage and Dissolution of Marriage Act (Senate Bill 57) http://www.ilga.gov/legislation/ilcs/ilcs3.asp?ActID=2086&ChapterID=59

Montenegro, X. P. American Association of Retired Persons (AARP) (May 2004). National Center for Family & Marriage Research at Bowling Green State University, Ohio. The Divorce Experience: A Study of Divorce at Midlife and Beyond. www.aarp.org

New York Post (June 25, 2015). Pope Francis: Divorce can be "morally necessary". http://nypost.com/2015/06/25/pope-francis-divorce

Psychology Today. (2012). https://www.psychologytoday.com/blog/buddy-system/201209/the-impact-divorce-friendships-couples-and-individuals

Statista, 2014. Personal acceptability of divorce in the United States. https://www.statista.com

Statista, 2016. American's moral stance towards divorce in 2016. www.statista.com/statistics/218524/americans-moral-stance-towards-divorce

Strohschein, L. Journal of Marriage and Family, December 2005; vol 67: pp 1286-1300.

Uniformed Services Former Spouses Protection Act (USFSOA) www.divorcesource.com/ds/military/usfspa-attention-must-be-paid-588.shtml

Know Your Divorce Options Before You Call an Attorney.

Contact Divorce Dimensions.

Dr. Ayala and her team of divorce professionals at Divorce Dimensions help couples and individuals who have decided to end their marriage with an uncontested or divorce pro se. For those couples able to forgo lengthy and costly litigation, we provide a graceful exit to marriage that is faster, affordable and simpler than the standard legal proceeding.

Call Divorce Dimensions toll free at 800-969-9087 to find out if an uncontested divorce in Cook, DuPage, Lake or Will County is right for you.

Divorce Dimensions Inc.
Navigating a path toward a healthier lifestyle.
Professional Divorce Services.

DivorceDimensions.com

"Growth that comes from positive change oftentimes leads to open doors, real solutions, and happiness."

- Doris N. Ayala

www.ingramcontent.com/pod-product-compliance
Lightning Source LLC
Chambersburg PA
CBHW070802050426
42452CB00012B/2463